A
CHRISTIAN'S
POCKET GUIDE
TO THE
CHINESE

OMF

CHRISTIAN
FOCUS

Copyright © OMF
www.omf.org.uk

ISBN 1-84550-315-5
ISBN 978-1-84550-315-4

10 9 8 7 6 5 4 3 2 1

Published in 2008
by
Christian Focus Publications,
Geanies House, Fearn,
Ross-shire, IV20 1TW Scotland

www.christianfocus.com

Cover design by Daniel Van Straaten

Printed by Nørhaven Paperback A/S, Denmark

Contents

One

FROM MAO TO MCDONALD'S – A NATION TRANSFORMED

The Wangfujing shopping centre is bustling with shoppers. A testimony to the growing materialism, wealth and Westernisation of Beijing, it is lined with expensive foreign boutiques, Starbucks coffee shops and McDonald's restaurants. Across China, old courtyards surrounded by traditional one- and two-storey houses have been ruthlessly demolished to make way for gleaming office blocks, hotels and shopping malls. Beijing is a prime example of the modernisation that is sweeping China.

Modern China is very different to that under Mao in the 1950s and 60s. In three decades the country has been transformed from a desperately poor, largely rural backwater to an economic powerhouse whose goods flood world markets and keep the US economy buoyant.

Though Mao's portrait still hangs over the gateway into the Forbidden City and his legacy of one-party dictatorship still remains in the form of periodic crackdowns on press and religious freedom, in all other ways China is a nation transformed.

In 2005 the Government admitted there were over 80,000 strikes, sit-downs and demonstrations across the country. Desperate to maintain 'stability and unity' at all costs, the central government has implemented various political crackdowns, but it seems unable to halt the steady, if slow, advance towards a more open civil society. Even if people are unable to express their grievances openly in the media, the widespread use of the internet and of mobile phones makes it increasingly difficult for the authorities to pretend injustices do not exist and to suppress dissent ruthlessly as in the days of Mao.

China is also experiencing a massive industrial revolution. While this took over a century in Europe, in China the transformation has occurred in just a few decades. At least 200 million rural workers have migrated into the cities in the last thirty years. China's influence on the world economy is rapidly increasing and its voracious appetite for raw materials such as oil and natural gas has led to agreements with countries in Central Asia and much further afield in Africa and South America. In the last 25 years China has increasingly opened its doors to international business and, in pursuit of economic growth, hundreds of thousands of educated Chinese have gone overseas to study. Tourists are also welcomed. Increasingly China is entering the world stage and the 2008 Olympic Games in Beijing serves as a showcase for immense patriotic pride in China's new-found affluence.

But this kind of explosive economic growth and exodus to the cities places a massive strain on key infrastructure such as schools, hospitals and social services. The rush to get rich and raise one's standard of living is natural – but has its downside.

Hundreds of millions of peasants and poor urban workers, mainly from uncompetitive state-controlled factories, are missing out on the new prosperity. Corrupt officials and land-developers seize the farms and villages of helpless peasants, creating an ever increasing divide between the rich and poor.

Spiritual Transformation

From 1966 until 1979 no places of worship were allowed anywhere in China. All churches were closed and religious expression suppressed. But since 1979 the Government has allowed Protestants to meet legally under the auspices of the party-supervised 'Three Self Patriotic Movement' and the China Christian Council. Over 55,000 churches and Christian groups now meet legally.

In 1949 there were just one million Protestants in the entire country. Today the Government admits there are some 20 million adults worshipping in state-controlled churches. Millions more meet in the ubiquitous house churches which have spread rapidly across the nation. No-one knows the true number of Christians in China but a conservative estimate would be 50-60 million Protestants and some 10-12 million Catholics.

The authorities are still trying to control the spread of Christianity, but with varying success. In some rural areas, persecution appears endemic, but in many places, even unregistered house churches meet with relatively few problems. There has been a vast change in the attitudes of ordinary Chinese towards Christianity. In the days of Mao, Christians were regarded with suspicion and hatred, as 'agents of imperialism' or even as 'counter-revolutionaries', but today many Chinese see Christianity as a force for good.

Students, Intellectuals And The Gospel

Today few Chinese know that Sun Yat-sen, the first President of the Chinese Republic in 1911, was a professing, baptised Christian. In the 1920s and 1930s the Communist Party secretly fostered a vast 'anti-Christian' movement that influenced many students and intellectuals. After 1949, under Mao, few educated young people even considered the Christian faith as an option.

It was the long agony of the Cultural Revolution (1966–76) which opened the eyes of many Chinese to the failings of Maoism. When Deng Xiaoping in 1978–79 'reversed the verdicts' of the party and declared the Cultural Revolution and Mao's extreme utopian policies a disaster, a huge spiritual vacuum was created. Since then many intellectuals have developed a keen interest in Christianity, believing it to be the source of Western culture and democracy – becoming 'culture Christians'.

Following the tragic events in June 1989, however, when the Government gunned down democracy activists in Beijing and other cities, many became disillusioned with Marxist ideology. The rhetoric sounded increasingly hollow and anachronistic and people began searching for real purpose and meaning in life. As a result, many intellectuals came to real faith in Christ.

Today, most Chinese universities have small Christian cell groups of both students and faculty members and in 2005 the party admitted that millions of its own members, who were supposedly keen atheists, were actually believers.

Search for Education – Search for Truth

Increasing numbers of Chinese are studying abroad. From the late 1970s the Government paid for many to study in foreign universities, so as to return to China and contribute to its 'Four Modernisation' programme. This began a flood of students and intellectuals arriving in universities and workplaces across the United States, UK, Australia, Singapore, France, Germany and many other countries.

Today the overwhelming majority of Chinese students studying abroad are self-funded, coming from a variety of affluent backgrounds. Many are children of party members and government officials who are up-and-coming entrepreneurs, academics and leaders. Even quite young children and teenagers are going overseas for short periods to study English. While these students are overseas they enjoy the novelty of full academic freedom without political constraint, and many are open to the gospel.

Carpe Diem – Seize the Day!

Currently there is unprecedented opportunity for Christians to befriend and witness to Chinese students and scholars living overseas. Never have they been so open to the gospel and many are aching for spiritual truth and asking deep questions about the role of Christianity. Not only are they looking for satisfactory solutions to personal problems, but also many serious Chinese intellectuals are looking to Christianity for long-lasting solutions to China's social and political crises. Superficial presentations of the gospel will not attract them, but genuine friendship and open, respectful debate will.

Although now we see spiritual openness and interest, Chinese political history is volatile and no one can foresee what the situation may be in five or ten years' time. Christians need to make the most of the opportunities we have now and the aim of this booklet is to help us understand Chinese culture and history, so we can befriend and reach out to the large number of Chinese passing through our towns and workplaces every day.

TWO

CHINESE STUDENTS IN PROFILE

Where Are They?

During the Cultural Revolution mindless egalitarianism meant that people regarded all intellectuals with suspicion. This period created a lack of qualified professionals and so since the 1980s the Chinese Government has been trying to remodel the education system to meet this need. As part of this improved education, from 1978 to 1998, the Chinese Government sent more than 190,000 scholars abroad to study. A large number of students have also independently headed to Western universities, funding their tuition themselves. Though the Government hoped most would return and contribute to China's efforts towards economic growth, they recently admitted that only one third have actually done so.

There are significant numbers of Mainland Chinese students in all major cities in the West. There are an estimated 150,000 Chinese currently in the UK with 50,000 new visas issued each year. There are equally large numbers in the USA, Canada, Japan, Australia,

Germany, France, Eastern Europe and Scandinavia. In addition many Chinese nurses are working in the Middle East, especially in the Gulf States.

Since 1998, the number of students studying abroad has dramatically increased and ranges from high school students to academics and professionals. Most boarding schools in the UK have some students from China doing A levels and going on to study at British universities. As the children of China's new wealthy businessmen, these young people are being given the best chance possible by their parents. The increasing numbers arriving in the UK have also been partly encouraged by a formal agreement between the UK and Chinese Governments that the UK will continue to issue 50,000 new visas a year for students from China to study in Britain. China prefers to send students to the UK because more of them return to China compared with those who study in the USA.

Who Are They?

The Chinese come from a very different environment and culture to that of a European or American. China has a highly regulated society, where high schools and universities have large classes, tight discipline and compulsory political study. School days are long and learning methods based on memorization. Arriving in the West, they enter the relatively liberal and amoral environment of a British university. Add on language difficulties, diet, weather, potential prejudice and discrimination and you will start to understand the massive culture shock.

Mainland Chinese culture is very different even from that of Hong Kong, Taiwanese, Singaporean or Malaysian Chinese. Westerners may tend to class all Chinese under the same umbrella, but the Chinese from China often do not relate well to Chinese from other countries. Many of the attitudes of Mainland Chinese are still influenced by Maoist Communism. Together with this are underlying traditional Chinese values, increasingly superimposed with materialism and a veneer of Westernisation. Many young Chinese arriving in the UK want to fit in with the undergraduate scene and so will become as Western as possible, but will remain very defensive at any criticism of China. A walk along any street in a major Chinese city shows this desire for Westernisation without losing their Chinese identity is now influencing them at home as well as abroad.

In previous years the majority of young people arriving in the West would have been the children of intellectuals or government officials and highly intelligent. Today, the ability of parents to pay for their children to study abroad regardless of academic ability is causing problems. Some universities accept students as long as they can afford the fees without considering if their English is good enough. Students sent to do A levels sometimes fail to get into a good university and so lose face with their Chinese peers and incur the wrath of their parents who are spending large sums of money on their education.

Categories of Students:

Mainland Chinese students fall roughly into the following categories:

(i)   Teenagers sent over by relatively wealthy parents to study at boarding school prior to doing their first degree at a UK university. Students educated in the Chinese high school system need to do a foundation course before starting university in Britain, so attending high school in the UK is thought to give them a better chance of getting into a good Western university. Obviously this is costly so most are from the top stratum of Chinese society.

(ii) Undergraduates who have obtained a place at a UK university while in China. Many universities have developed special links with certain cities or universities in China and send representatives there to 'sell' their courses. The number of these students is increasing rapidly and they are in many ways more difficult to contact – many want to enter fully into the 'student scene' and do not want to be involved in minority activities, while others simply have little time for extra-curricular activities. This means there is an even greater need for Christian undergraduates to take opportunities to befriend them and share the gospel with them.

(iii) Professors, lecturers, postgraduates, post-doctoral research students and visiting scholars. Those in their late twenties and early thirties were only children when the Tiananmen incident took place in 1989, so unlike their elders who had been through the Cultural Revolution, many of these students have had a much easier life. Ten years ago a non-Christian Chinese here with his wife and young daughter was afraid to allow his daughter to attend Sunday School 'because it is not allowed in China'. Now most Chinese, unless they have come into contact with Christianity in China, would not even know such a regulation exists and in many cases would be unaware of the pressures on religious groups in China.

(iv) Special groups e.g. those sent to learn English in preparation for the Beijing Olympics; groups of teachers on summer courses and so on.

Although these Chinese students are here in large numbers, those able to study here represent a very small minority of the total student population in China and the country as a whole. They are the most privileged amongst their Chinese peers, but as the only child of doting parents, some may not recognise the fact.

Their Attitudes To Study

Mainland Chinese students have a reputation for studying hard and taking life seriously. Some students arriving in the West are still acutely aware that they form an intellectual elite and are under pressure to excel. Some have a genuine desire to build up their country, but many are intent on furthering their own careers. They are not lacking in ambition and are now more than able to compete with Westerners for the best graduate jobs.

In recent years however, more and more students have adopted an increasingly relaxed attitude. Those wanting to identify with the Western student lifestyle often pay less attention to their work and those from more privileged backgrounds may be less diligent about studying, as their parents are paying their fees and they have not had to worry much about grades. A professor in Beijing commented recently that the current generation of Chinese students was the most apathetic he'd ever come across – hearing this comment, a statistics lecturer at a UK university said, 'I have them in my first year class. They are totally different to previous Chinese students, much more like Western ones, late for class, late handing in work and keen to party!' Western Christians can have a positive impact simply through being conscientious about their own work.

Some of those students, however, who have been accepted by some of the universities on their ability to pay rather than their academic ability have struggled with their work, lost their confidence and feel let down and used.

Their Lifestyle

Chinese scholars abroad who are supported by government funding tend to live simply. The majority of these receive fairly modest funding which allows for tuition fees, board and a small amount of pocket money. Some find it very hard to make ends meet and take part time jobs. It is very common to find the scholar's spouse working in a Chinese restaurant or takeaway or in one of the growing number of Chinese medicine shops.

It may be a different story for students who are funded by their parents. Some of these may be fairly well-off and well able to live a lifestyle comparable to their British peers. While some are conscious of the hard work and sacrifices of their parents, others take their opportunities for granted and will freely email or call home asking for more money.

Although many of the younger students want to appear Western and part of the student scene, they often struggle with the lack of morals and the heavy drinking common across the UK. China is changing fast in this respect but its society as a whole is still much more conservative than in the West. Twenty-five years ago it was uncommon to see a young couple even walking arm in arm in public. Many students who outwardly join in with the lifestyle of UK students may inwardly feel guilty about their behaviour as they know their parents would disapprove. It is also important to remember that while they want to appear Western they are much more patriotic than the average British student and will generally not accept any criticism of China by a non-Chinese.

One thing Chinese students love doing is going on the internet and chatting to friends online. English language blog and chat websites such as www.myspace.com and www.facebook.com may be good places to catch up with Chinese you have started to befriend.

Christians can have a major impact if their own life-style cuts across the rampant materialism of the

West. If we are aware of the evils of our own society, such as commercial exploitation, inflated advertising and pornography, then we can meet with many of our Chinese friends on common ground.

Often Chinese students, even those with families, will live together in cheap rented housing or in university accommodation, spending much of their free time as a group. In order to befriend them, you may have to take the initiative and should not be put off by what seems a rather tight knit group mentality. Many are keen to meet British people and improve their English, so will be very willing to make friends. If you have been to China, telling them about your time there and your appreciation of Chinese culture may be a good starting point.

Chinese living outside main cities or university towns, where few other Chinese are based, often feel very lonely. The importance of welcoming newcomers as soon as they arrive in the West, and showing them genuine love and hospitality, cannot be overemphasised. Most will suffer from severe culture shock, so a friendly welcome will help ease them into their new life overseas.

> Many universities have international welcome programmes just before the start of the academic year. Even if you are not a student, why not see if you can get involved, or start an international welcome group at your church?

Things Chinese seem to like about Britain, America and other English-speaking countries include the air quality and cleanliness. Things they dislike tend to include the weather and the food. Some Mainland Chinese will be completely unprepared for cooking by themselves: in Chinese homes their parents will have cooked for them and at Chinese universities everyone eats together in canteens, with minimal facilities for self-catering.

> If you're a student in a catered hall of residence, the dining hall is a really good place to build up relationships with Mainland Chinese people. Try inviting them out for dinner. A Guangdong or Cantonese restaurant will be the closest to the Chinese food those from southern China are used to, while those from the north may prefer a Beijing restaurant, and those from the west of China the spicy food of a Sichuan restaurant. Much of the food served in Chinese restaurants and takeaways here is fairly Westernised compared with what is eaten in China but your Chinese friend may appreciate the thought. It may even result in them offering to cook you a proper Chinese meal!

Their Pressures

To the Chinese, many Westerners may seem material-istic, selfish, lazy and overly individualistic. Living and studying in such an alien environment can cause tensions for them. Though it is less common these days, some of the Chinese arriving in the West still have wives and families back in China, whom they may not be able to see for as long as two or three years, if they do not have the money to return home for a visit. It is more common now for the couple to come together, but this is not always the case. Young people may be separated from their parents for equally long periods. Sometimes parents are able to come over for up to a six-month period, but this, of course, is limited to those with means, able to afford the accommodation and time off work.

Often it is a man who has come to the West because of his job or studies, so the accompanying wives of students and professionals can feel very isolated. Though intellectuals, they may have limited spoken English and find it hard to get a satisfying job. While the man will become part of an office or academic department, working long hours, steadily improving his language and engaging with others, his wife may have a menial job and find it difficult to practise her English. This will compound her feelings of isolation and make her in even greater need of friendship.

Most are able to adapt to varying degrees, but seemingly simple things like adjusting to Western food can add difficulty to what is an already pressurised and stressful transition. The fact that a few have been known to commit suicide shows that these pressures are very real.

Students and Chinese Politics

China is still a highly politicised society dominated by the Chinese Communist Party. During the Cultural Revolution and its aftermath, politics took precedence over intellectual ability. Better a slow socialist train than a fast capitalist one. Better to be politically 'Red' than technically 'expert'. Now the pendulum has swung the other way, with a much stronger emphasis on being 'expert'. But this does not mean that political attitudes count for nothing. Being a member of the

Communist Party is a smart career move but it means that person is not allowed to have a religion.

In the past, party membership was a major issue for those who wanted to become Christians. The party has relaxed some of its policies on religion and more people are willing to leave the party for their faith. But in recent years the party has had drives to purge universities of Christians, and its own ranks of committed religious believers. A really committed Christian is still unlikely to rise very far in terms of position, even academically.

Some believers will not have openly professed their faith in China, and will be unwilling to do so while abroad, but many Mainland Chinese will be totally unaware of potential pressures for them if they become Christians. Talking to them about persecution of Christians in China will produce puzzled stares and denial that any such thing could happen – 'Those things happened during the Cultural Revolution but not now'. Helping them be more aware will need sensitive explanation and an acknowledgement that China is a huge country and what is true in one place will not be so in another. The best solution is to try to find a Chinese Christian who can talk with them. Others may be aware of the situation but are embarrassed by Western criticism and the loss of face for their country, and will not want to discuss it.

Unlike those living abroad during the Cultural Revolution, today very few Chinese will wish to prop-agate Chinese Communism, but it is still unwise to criticise China's present leadership or party policies.

Political subjects are not taboo though, particularly if a close friendship is formed, and occasionally a Chinese person may come out with criticisms themselves in private. Such criticism should never be shared with other Chinese scholars and you should never engage in delicate political discussions with a group of Chinese, in case one of them says something in front of the others which he may later regret.

It is worth noting that all university students in Mainland China must study Chinese Communist Thought as part of their degrees and the marks go towards their final grades. If you are talking to a graduate educated in China they will have been taught the 'correct' opinions on Chinese history and politics. You may hear the same opinions again and again whether the individuals agrees with them or not. Particularly sensitive topics to avoid include the status of Taiwan and Tibet. Many Chinese, even intellectuals, are patriotic and accept the party's views on these controversial issues.

Chinese embassies abroad do sometimes still attempt to monitor scholars, and there may occasionally be informants who report back. It is wise not to encourage scholars to take part in activities which might get them into trouble with the Chinese Embassy. Scholars have much more freedom of movement abroad than they did but there is still a long way to go. We should be sensitive to our Chinese friends' situations overseas and to the changing political climate back home. If a Chinese friend who has been coming to church fairly regularly should suddenly stop, there may well be a good reason, and we should think of alternative and sensitive ways to keep up the friendship.

Three

HOW TO MAKE FRIENDS

Those who work or study at universities or colleges with Mainland Chinese have tremendous opportunities to get to know them. But simple activities like going to local coffee shops and internet cafes, attending sports clubs or other events may give you a chance to meet and chat with Mainland Chinese living in your area.

> Remember to treat your friend as a friend, and one for whom Christ died. Do not, whatever you do, make them your pet 'project'. Jesus never treated anyone this way and neither should we. God created them and gave them dignity; treating them as a merely another potential notch on the inside of our Bible cover is to fail to 'love them as we love ourselves'.

As friends though, we should be looking for opportunities to speak to them about Christ. The key to doing this is prayer. We must trust the Lord to guide us to the right person at the right time. Prayer for guidance and wisdom is vital, and continued prayer will be absolutely essential if we expect to see lasting spiritual fruit.

When it is still impossible for Westerners to work openly in China as missionaries, we have amazing opportunities to meet Mainland Chinese on our door-step. Let us show them the love of Christ.

What You Can Do Together

No-one can prescribe how to develop a friendship but here are some suggestions of activities you could try to help develop your friendships with Mainland Chinese:

- Invite them to a meal at home with your family
- Practise English conversation, or offer to help them if they should need it, for example with the shopping, or with a visit to the doctor, hospital or local government offices, or perhaps in filling in forms or writing letters
- If you have the time, offer to 'proofread' a student's work or thesis
- Accept an invitation to eat a Chinese meal with them and/or to learn how to cook Chinese dishes. Go to a Chinese supermarket with them and help buy ingredients
- Take them to the seaside or visit the botanical gardens or any beauty spot. Even a garden or DIY centre or a car boot sale is unusual and so interesting for them
- Visit places of historical interest such as palaces, castles, museums and old churches
- Go on a holiday or trip together. Camping or staying in a youth hostel can keep the cost down
- Visit bookshops, especially second hand ones, to help them get hold of cheap English

language textbooks, English literature and technical books. You might also give English magazines to women, and children's books or Bible colouring books to children

- Visit a school or hospital. These are likely to be very different from those in China and will be of cultural interest
- Invite them to a Christian wedding
- Introduce mothers to a church-based 'Mums and Toddlers' group
- Take them to a café – Starbucks is a growing culture in Mainland China
- Watch a Chinese film with them. For some recommendations see http://www.hongkonglegends.co.uk

Beware of taking Mainland Chinese to a pub. It is quite an alien situation for them, but they may appreciate the cultural experience. Just remember they will not know what to do – how to order drinks, or the purpose in sitting there etc – so choose somewhere less crowded and with space to talk.

- Watch a football match together. A lot of Mainland Chinese men love the English Premiership which is shown every Saturday night on Chinese TV. Invite them to play a game or join a local team with you
- Ask them to teach you some Chinese games – Chinese chess or Go are well-known in China
- Show them photos of your family and ask them about theirs
- Offer to read a book or newspaper together to help them with their English

In some towns there is an 'English Corner' where a group of Christians invite international people to make friends and practise their English. This will also give the opportunity to introduce foreigners to other Christians. English Corners are a Mainland Chinese invention that has been adapted by Western Christians and so will be familiar to most Chinese. Most Chinese enjoy these events as they offer less pressurised social contact, help them with their language, and provide the chance for Chinese families to get to know each other. It also creates an arena in which questions can be asked and some who have run these groups have found themselves fielding serious spiritual questions.

It is really worth introducing new Chinese friends to Chinese Christians you know, even if they are not from Mainland China. It will show that Christianity is not just for Westerners and a Chinese Christian may well be able to help answer difficult or sensitive questions in a more relevant way. In the UK there are many Chinese churches and fellowships. Increasingly they are reaching out to Mainland Chinese and holding Mainland Chinese fellowship groups, Bible studies or special events in Mandarin.

Invitations to the home are especially appreciated. Some Chinese spend years in the West without ever being invited into a family home. In a book written by a Chinese scholar returning to China a student described the highlight of his entire time abroad as being a long conversation on a long-distance bus with a friendly Westerner. What an indictment of our unfriendly, self-centred and over-individualistic culture. Some people feel unwilling to 'spoil' Christmas or Thanksgiving celebrations by inviting foreigners into the family, but many people living abroad will spend Christmas alone. By inviting them to our homes we can show genuine friendship and can share the love of Christ.

If you live in an area where there are no Chinese students you can still befriend them by offering hospitality through the HOST programme (see contact details at back) which finds placements for students who want to spend a short holiday in a British home.

Many people feel very awkward when trying to interact with people from other cultures. You should be sensitive to difference but do realise that minor mistakes and misunderstandings are bound to happen. Just be relaxed and apologise. A Chinese person will most likely be more than willing to forgive. After all, they have to deal with cultural differences as much as you do. We might find it tricky to use chopsticks; the Chinese find it just as strange to master knives and forks. Ask them to explain Chinese etiquette, and then explain our Western table manners to them.

Remember that people's requests and interests will vary considerably. An all-rounded, holistic approach to forming cross-cultural friendships is best rather than a narrow concentration on purely 'spiritual' activities. Let them see Christians enjoying life in its fullness and, hopefully, seeing the difference Christ makes to a person in a variety of circumstances. As friendship is a two way affair, we should seek to learn from them and to appreciate the richness of Chinese culture.

Four

MEETING THEM WHERE THEY ARE

'The double disavowal by which both [Confucianism and Maoist Communism] have been successively rejected has left an emptiness at the heart of Chinese metaphysical life – the life of meanings – that no mixture of consumerism and familism, power, list and patriotism, borrowed modernism or neo-Confucian revivalism, will fill satisfactorily for long.'

Changing Stories in the Chinese World,
Mark Elvin, Standford University Press, 1998

Despite cultural and political differences and the many barriers there may be in presenting the gospel to them, Chinese people are in need of Christ and his salvation as much as anyone. As with everyone, there will be those who show no interest, those who for various reasons are willing to listen and discuss, and those who seem ready to respond.

You Don't Have To Be A High-Flier

'When I came to you, brothers, I did not come with eloquence or superior wisdom as I proclaimed to you the testimony about God. For I resolved to know nothing while I was with you except Jesus Christ and him crucified. I came to you in weakness and fear, and with much trembling. My message and my preaching were not with wise and persuasive words, but with a demonstration of the Spirit's power, so that your faith might not rest on men's wisdom, but on God's power.'

Paul the Apostle, 1 Corinthians 2:1-5

A love for Christ and for people are essential in witnessing. Don't underestimate how much someone will respond to genuine love and friendship. You don't need to be an intellectual high-flier to offer friendship.

If you do have some knowledge of subjects such as science or Chinese Marxism though, you will be more able to give a reasoned case for what you believe, and to talk with the more able students. To help you answer any questions, OMF has produced a series of booklets, CDs and tapes specially for Mainland Chinese intellectuals. Some titles are in Mandarin and English. These cover a range of questions which may arise in your friend's mind. The Jesus Video in Mandarin and the European edition of the bi-monthly Overseas Campus Magazine produced in the USA by Chinese Christian intellectuals are both useful tools. See the Appendix for details of where to order them. You don't need to be an expert to pass on a resource that will be really useful.

English Christian books and videos can also be used effectively and could be a way to help the Chinese person improve their English at the same time.

Some Useful Background

For over 50 years China has been ruled by the militantly atheistic Communist Party. During the Cultural Revolution all churches were closed and most Bibles destroyed. In the last 20 years over 40 million Bibles and New Testaments and a limited range of other Christian books have been published within China, but many people are still unable to obtain them. And because the party controls the press and the publishing houses, all books and magazines on public sale have been written within a general Marxist framework and with party approval.

To a greater or lesser extent everyone in China has been influenced by Marxism, even the intellectuals who oppose it. Most people have been brought up in the Marxist education system, and so will have been indoctrinated from kindergarten up through university. Religion has no place in this system except as an object of derision and an outmoded superstition. Unless they have Christian relatives, students are unlikely to have anything more than a vague awareness of Christianity.

Attitudes towards religion are gradually changing though in academic circles. Articles have appeared in sociological journals admitting its positive influence. Some Chinese may have visited churches out of curiosity. But many books and journals still churn out negative images of Christianity and of religion as the 'opiate of the people'.

In befriending Chinese, it is not the aim to defend the Western way of life nor to attack the more objectionable aspects of life in China. There are plenty of things wrong in our society which are glaringly obvious to our Chinese friends, but usually they are too polite to point them out. We should be trying to point them to Jesus Christ's values rather than those of a particular society.

Bourgeois Religion

Chinese Communism took on all the virulent atheism of Soviet Communism. The writings of Marx, Engels, Lenin and Stalin are still the 'sacred books' of Chinese Communism, together with those of Mao Zedong. Indeed the official ideology sports the cumbersome title of 'Marxism Leninism Mao Zedong Thought'.

Marx regarded all religion as 'the opiate of the people'. Lenin went further calling the very idea of God 'unutterable vileness'. Mao himself, from his own experience of Chinese folk religion among the peasants, regarded religion as an evil and as one of the 'four thick ropes binding the Chinese people' (i.e. keeping them in bondage). In a textbook he helped write in 1939, Christian missionary work was classified as 'cultural aggression' of Western imperialism 'poisoning the minds of the Chinese people'.

In more recent times, under Deng Xiaoping, ideology tended to take a back seat, though it was never dismissed. These days few Chinese really believe in it, but many go through the motions, often only in order to join the party and obtain a good position with perks. Young people are starting to see Mao in a more favourable light, as they are encouraged to focus on the positive aspects of his rule.

Since the Cultural Revolution began, academics have been passed through many political programmes to remould them and rid them of 'bourgeois' and 'reactionary' ways of thought. They will have learnt to keep their own thoughts very private and to be wary of expressing opinions which could be construed as opposing the party. Though these attitudes are no longer promoted with the same vigour, such ingrained behaviours are not easily dropped, so many Chinese, even when abroad, will continue to express few individual opinions. Some younger students arriving in the West, however, are starting to relish their freedom and be more outspoken.

Will Religion Naturally Die?

According to Marxist dogma, all religion will wither away naturally as supposedly scientific and dialectical materialist Marxism triumphantly advances. The question for Chinese Marxists is whether it should be left to die of its own accord, or forcibly suppressed.

The former policy of allowing religion to head for natural extinction was adopted in the early fifties. But even then, by 1958 most churches had been closed and many pastors such as Wang Mingdao sent to labour camps. During the Cultural Revolution period (1966–76) when Mao and the extreme left-wing 'Gang of Four' brought the entire nation to the brink of catastrophe, all churches were closed and all overt expressions of Christianity (as well as other religions) totally suppressed. Mao died in 1976. In 1979 after Deng Xiaoping came to power China rapidly opened up to the outside world and embarked on a programme of economic modernisation. The party deliberately reverted to its 'softer' line on religion; in 1979 churches, temples and mosques were reopened across the country. Today there are over 55,000 legally registered Protestant churches. However they are supervised, with varying degrees of surveillance, by the government-controlled Three Self Patriotic Movement (TSPM). This ostensibly stands for the self-government, self-support and self-propagation of the church – all laudable Biblical principles. In actual fact, the TSPM is controlled by the State Administration for Religious Affairs (SARA) and the United Front Work Department of the Communist Party, the police and other party and government organs. Despite the efforts of a small clique of politically minded church leaders at the top who compromise with the party, at grass-roots level the overwhelming majority of the Christians are fervently evangelical as are most of the pastors. Despite the best efforts of the party to crack down periodically, the gospel has exploded across the country – from about one million Christians in 1949 to over fifty million today – and the movement of the Holy Spirit is evident not just in the massive growth of the unregistered house-churches but also in many of the above-ground State (TSPM) churches as well.

Freedom of Religion?

This limited religious toleration does not mean that the party has given its approval to the spread of the gospel.

Far from it. The present limited 'freedom of religious belief' is a deliberate concession aimed at uniting all people in China, so that all are supporting the party and behind the policy of economic modernisation. The freedom only extends to 'normal' religious activities sanctioned by the party and practised within the four walls of government registered TSPM churches.

Persecution of Christians

The majority of Chinese Christians worship privately in homes, or in semi-public gatherings often spontaneously organised. They face harassment and sometimes arrest. In January 1994 new religious legislation was signed by Premier Li Peng himself, calling for strict registration of all religious meeting places. This strict registration was reinforced in much more detailed Religious Regulations published by the Government in March 2005. Over the last few years hundreds of Christian house church evangelists and believers have been arrested, fined and imprisoned for preaching the gospel outside the strict limits laid down by the atheistic government. Most are eventually released, but some have been sent to serve long prison sentences in labour camps.

Chinese Problems with Christianity

Jesus was a myth
Many books recently published in China on religious matters, state categorically that Jesus never existed, but that he was a myth created out of the specific social conditions existing in Palestine in the first century AD.

They also dismiss the Bible as a collection of Jewish and early Christian stories.

Helpful Resources:

More Than a Carpenter, Josh McDowell, Kingsway, ISBN 978-1-84291-265-2

Ancient Evidence for the Life of Jesus, Gary Habermas, College Press Publishing, ISBN 978-0-89900-732-8

The Birth of Christianity: The First Twenty Years, Paul Barnett, Eerdmans Publishing, ISBN 978-0-80282-781-4

The creation question

A crude form of atheistic evolutionism is still taught throughout the Chinese educational system. The Communist Party seems unaware that few scientists in the West still hold with 19th century materialistic Darwinism, and that many have moved on to positions more open to the possibility of creation and of the existence of God. If you are trying to understand and share with Chinese friends it will be helpful to have some understanding of the science/religion and creation/evolution debates.

A word of caution: a dogmatic approach that insists that the world was created 5,000 or 10,000 years ago may not be helpful. While firmly stating the case for creation and the existence of God we should always remember that our aim is to lead friends to faith in Christ, and not place even more intellectual stumbling blocks in their path over which evangelical Christians themselves differ.

Helpful Resources:

Darwin's Black Box, Michael Behe, Simon & Schuster Inc, ISBN 978-0-68483-493-1

Darwin on Trial, P Johnson, IVP, ISBN 978-0-83081-758-0

The Wedge of Truth, P Johnson, IVP, ISBN 978-0-83082-395-6

The Creator and the Cosmos, Hugh Ross, Navpress, ISBN 978-1-57683-288-2

The New Flatlanders, Eric Middleton, Highland Books, ISBN 978-1-89791-365–9

Why wasn't Galileo listened to?

Another criticism often raised by Chinese scholars concerns Galileo and the reactionary Catholic Church. Galileo was gagged by the Inquisition as he defended the then new theory that the earth revolved around the sun. It took the Vatican some 300 years to lift their ban.

While in no way wishing to excuse the Roman Catholic Church's actions, we can point out that scholars agree that the facts of the case are not simple. We can also let our Chinese friends know the considerable contribution of Protestant Christianity and Puritanism to the development of the natural sciences in Europe. Why did science make such huge leaps in Protestant northern Europe in the 16th and 17th centuries but languish in ancient Greece and China? Food for thought for our Chinese friends.

Helpful Resources:

The Galileo Connection, Charles Hummel, IVP, ISBN 978-0-87784-500-3

Religion and the Rise of Modern Science, R Hookyaas, Regent College Publishing, ISBN 978-1-57383-018-8

Thinking Through Chinese Communist Thought

Little has been published on how Christians should approach Chinese Communist thought though the following questions may be helpful to think through and consider from a Mainland Chinese perspective. I'm not suggesting that these topics should be raised with all Mainland Chinese, but even if you don't discuss them, these questions may help you understand the environment and thought patterns of those brought up in China, start a Chinese person thinking or bring about relevant discussions.

- What is truth? Is it relative or absolute? Can the Party define and change it? If so, does yesterday's truth become today's lie?
- What is human nature? Can it be changed by force, manipulation or propaganda? Is it possible to produce a Maoist or Marxist 'new man' through coercion? Mao tried to change people's motivation so that they would genuinely 'serve the people' but didn't he ultimately fail? Is there a higher, inner motivation? Christians believe in a spiritual new birth.
- Can evil be seen totally in class terms of exploited and exploiter, proletarian and capitalist? Is this too simplistic? Did it not lead to monstrous injustice and suffering during the Cultural Revolution, when people were

punished solely for their class background, for example if their grandfather was a landlord? Is the Christian doctrine of original sin not more realistic and in tune with reality than shallow, optimistic humanism?

- Are science and technology, that is, the Four Modernisations of science, industry, agriculture and defence, the answer to China's and the world's problems? Why are delinquency, divorce, drug abuse and suicide rates so high in the 'advanced' countries of America, Europe and Japan? Note: China is fast catching up on some of these!

- Is something more needed to solve these problems than science and education?

- What value has the individual? Is it only as part of 'the masses' or the party? Are people only gifted animals produced by blind evolutionary forces?

- Is materialism true to reality? How can we explain the reality of sacrificial love? Doesn't materialism quench the human spirit? Where were the great works of art and literature in the Soviet Union and Mao's China? The Cultural Revolution actually destroyed Chinese culture (burning books, works of art, ancient temples etc). Christianity has, in contrast, inspired some of the world's greatest art and music.

- Is Christianity superstition? If so, why do Christians so strongly oppose astrology, worship of idols and fortune telling? What is the difference between true and false religion? Is Christianity only a reactionary tool of the exploiting classes? Most of Jesus' disciples were humble, working people and the early Christians were from the 'lower' classes, even slaves. For three hundred years the early church was persecuted. Although wicked men have perverted Christ's teachings, true Christianity has inspired much social improvement: education, hospitals, the abolition of the slave trade (Wilberforce, UK), and the abolition of harsh factory conditions (Lord Shaftesbury, UK). The eighteenth century Methodist revival transformed British society.

- Is the Marxist analysis accurate that religion will die out? In China the government admits that the church is growing rapidly and even has a special name for the revival: 'Christianity fever'. Is there not a spiritual and ideological vacuum causing many in China to become Christians?

- Why has Christianity grown rapidly in the Third World though all the countries in Africa, Asia and South America are no longer under colonial rule? Christianity is not just a 'Western' religion and was actually founded in Asia.

- When did Christianity first come to China? Not with the gunboats in the nineteenth century as many Chinese believe, but it was brought by Nestorian Persian monks in the seventh century AD. The Nestorian Tablet in the museum

in Xian is historical proof of the very early date (AD 635) when Nestorians first arrived in China.
- Was Christ just a myth? The gospels were written very soon after his death and resurrection. Christianity is a historically based religion, based on Jesus Christ himself.
- Is not the Christian the true revolutionary? Christians are not motivated by class hatred but by love; they try to conform neither to capitalist nor Communist society.
- True Christianity (unlike Buddhism) is world-affirming, not world-denying and escapist. True Christians seek to make a positive contribution to society.

Questions Chinese are Asking

Mainland Chinese have many questions, many of which they are uncomfortable asking other Chinese and will only feel free to share with their Western friends. Here are some they have asked in recent years:

'Since the Beijing massacre (4 June 1989) I have lost all faith in the party: but what is there to put in its place?'

'Christianity is really a Western religion, isn't it?'

'I am shocked to discover that some quite intelligent people in England believe in God despite the fact that science and the theory of evolution have disproved God. This is a material world, so how can man have a soul?'

'Where do I look for God; in the realm of idealism or realism?'

'I have been badly let down by one "Saviour", Chairman Mao, who finished as a broken idol criticised for his mistakes. I could not bear it if Jesus were to prove an idol, too. I could not go through this again; it would break my heart.'

'I have always believed that Christians are imperialists, reactionaries and rogues but those who truly befriend me in this country are all Christians. Why?'

'If there is a God, why does he allow evil?'

'Why are there so many churches? What is the difference between Protestantism and Roman Catholicism?'

'Why did God send Jesus as a Jew? Why not a Chinese, as our culture goes back thousands of years?'

'I believe all you are telling me about Jesus is true but in my head it is like there is a tape recorder saying "There is no God, there is no God".'

'First I need to make myself a better person then I will become a Christian'

'Do young people in the West have empty hearts like we do?'

Five

WITNESSING TO MAINLAND CHINESE

There is no one approach that will work for all. Much depends on the relationship of trust and friendship already built up. Superficial evangelistic techniques, such as bombardment with Bible texts or simplistic presentations of the 'ABCs' of the gospel are likely to leave people bemused, and be seen as distasteful. After all, they are not so far removed from the manipulative techniques used by the Red Guards during the Cultural Revolution, which are anathema to Chinese students. A student approached by Jehovah's Witnesses soon after her arrival in UK as an undergraduate finally gave up attending their meetings partly because she did not like them telling her she had to believe what they were saying.

Pray for patience and discernment in knowing the right moment to present that aspect of the gospel most suited to your friend's particular needs. We need to cultivate the art of listening.

> Remember: Treat your friend as a friend. Do not, whatever you do, make them your pet 'project'.

With some, an indirect approach may be best at first. The great Christian festivals, especially Christmas and Easter, present ideal opportunities for inviting students and their families to carol services and other Christian activities where there will be a clear gospel message. Most Mainland Chinese will feel easy about coming to such important 'cultural' events even if they never attend church at other times. Many have a keen interest in all aspects of Western culture, including religion.

Some have visited churches and Christian student groups out of curiosity, but others need to be gently encouraged, and in ways that will not immediately alienate them. Some will feel happier to come to a church or to any other Christian meeting if they can later tell their Embassy or colleagues that they went out of interest in the host culture or customs. Do not give up trying just because some always politely refuse, or just don't turn up having accepted verbally.

One excellent way of encouraging international friends is to arrange a meal or other activity for a particular professional group, such as doctors, scientists or engineers. The speaker should be a Christian and a qualified and respected member of that profession. They will attract greater interest than a Christian minister who will be expected to talk about Christianity. It may be wiser to hold such functions for international students generally, rather than specifically for Chinese; they will feel less conspicuous that way.

If you are inviting husbands and wives, then some activity should be provided for children, who always accompany their parents on such occasions. Baby-sitting is a foreign concept to the Chinese.

There is no reason why Chinese friends should not be invited to church and you will naturally want to take them to your own church and introduce them to the fellowship there. However it will also be helpful at some stage to take them along to churches with other styles of worship and in different styles of building as this will help them to understand that Christianity is not dependent on the external setting or forms of worship. But do your homework first, a vast Gothic cathedral with perhaps a small, relatively elderly congregation may be of great cultural interest to them, and may raise questions. However, going to a cathedral service (depending on the cathedral!) may confirm their belief that Christianity is dying out just as the Marxists say. Such buildings have curiosity value, particularly if the person has only had contact with Buddhism or folk religion in China, but could give a false impression of Christianity. A more modern church service filled with young people will challenge such assumptions. Experience of a variety of styles of church worship is also a tremendous help for those who become Christians and then return to China and need to fit in to a different style of church there.

Meetings on campus or in the home may have more impact than those in a more 'churchy' environment. Introduce your friend to Christians after the service or meeting, but remember not everyone will be sensitive

to the background and beliefs of a Mainland Chinese.
Many assume that they are Christian and talk about
the persecution of Christians in China which will
either baffle or offend them.

> Once when I took a Chinese friend to church, someone very kindly
> came up to welcome the newcomer. However, on learning the in-
> dividual was from China, they launched into a belligerent dia-
> tribe against Communism. Situations like this are best avoided!

Chinese children who are in local schools could be
invited to Sunday School or mid-week Christian clubs.
Children are usually very open to Christian teaching.

Many churches now have pastorates, congrega-
tions, study groups, cells and evangelistic courses
specially designed for international students, and
some even have groups specifically for Chinese or
East Asians. Ask around your local churches to see
what's on offer.

If Your Friend Shows Spiritual Interest

It is exciting when a non-Christian shows interest in
the gospel, but don't then tell everyone in your church.
News gets around and could cause difficulties for
your friend. It is advisable to preserve confidentiality
by telling only a few friends who will pray. Some
Chinese will be frightened that the embassy will find
out about their interest or new faith so we must respect
their feelings. If they live with other Chinese students
it may be better not to talk about spiritual things at
their home, but to meet at your home instead.

To become a Christian is a very serious decision which could bring pressures upon them if they return to China, and may, even now, cause them difficulties. Talk honestly with them about the cost of discipleship. By all means give them Bibles and good Christian literature which will help them. (English/Chinese bilingual Bibles and literature are available from OMF. See the Appendix for further details). Suggest doing a Bible study, perhaps on a weekly basis, and make it easy for them to invite their other friends if they want to. Encourage them to take a Bible and a few Christian books, tapes or videos back with them if they return to China.

Many, many Mainland Chinese have found Christ while abroad and been baptised. Baptism may have serious consequences if discovered by the authorities, so raise the subject sensitively and talk through every aspect thoroughly. It is especially important to ensure the person understands what repentance means. Although China is considered atheist and Communist, things such as idols, lucky charms and ancestor worship are still prevalent in the background of their culture. Individuals' involvement may have been 'innocent' in that it was culture-based and routine rather than spiritual belief, but the Chinese may need help in dealing with and understanding their involvement in these traditions and finding freedom in Christ. (Please contact the OMF Ethnic Minstries Team if you need help and advice in dealing with these issues.) Ironically, most will also need to be warned of the need for care when they return to

China. As discussed earlier, those not in contact with Christianity in China may be completely unaware of the problems Christians face.

If your friend wants to be baptised, help your minister and church leaders to grasp the need for sensitivity. Western ministers often find it difficult to put themselves in the shoes of someone returning to an authoritarian society and may also not understand the need to deal with any spiritual issues as described above.

Follow-Up

Follow-up of Chinese people who turn to Christ is not easy and there is no tailor-made solution. The following are some suggestions:

Those with experience in helping returnees in China have said that the most helpful thing we can do is to disciple the person while they are in the UK. Teaching them what it means to serve, giving them opportunities to do so rather than always being on the receiving end and familiarising them with as many different churches and styles of worship as possible will make the transition home easier.

Remember to email or write to your friends after they go back to China. The authorities accept that people who study overseas make friends there. But be aware that all mail is monitored and may be opened. Email, unless it's secure, is also easy for the authorities to spy on. Your friends may write freely of Christian things or may avoid mentioning them, but follow their lead. Ask them how happy they are to talk freely about Christianity before they return but don't forget that they may not realise the potential difficulties.

You could try and agree abbreviations for common words before they leave but it may be better just to agree that you will write about Christian things without using overtly Christian language. E.g. 'All our friends were thinking of you when we met up last weekend,' instead of 'We were praying for you in church last Sunday'. Words such as God, Bible, Christian, faith, prayer, Jesus, Holy Spirit, missionary, baptise, and worship will all attract attention if written in an email or in a letter which may be opened and checked. Don't be clever and write in code though as this will make the authorities particularly suspicious.

A Christmas card and the occasional letter with family news and so on will be greatly appreciated by friends back in China. If your letters are not answered, do not be too disappointed. Your friend could have received them and decided not to write back, but the letter may never even have arrived. Intellectuals in China are very mobile and change their addresses frequently.

Communication by telephone, mobile phone (including text message), or email is like sending a postcard – it can easily be read and monitored by others. The Chinese Government has thousands of employees whose sole job is to read and monitor emails before they reach the intended recipient. The same care is needed when writing a letter.

The best follow-up, if possible, is a personal visit but make sure this is really wanted by your friend (possibly by getting a third party to check for you as your friend may not want to say no to you) and will not embarrass them or cause difficulties.

What About Attending Church In China?

This is quite a tricky area and there is no easy answer. Some scholars may wish to attend a TSPM church, but they should be aware that they may be monitored and their names passed back to their university or work unit as a newly returned scholar showing great interest in Christianity. Services at Christmas and Easter attract less attention. Others may wish to attend house churches, but this can be difficult to arrange. To put them in touch with a house church or study group, you really need to have Christian contacts in the city they're returning to. This in itself is often complicated and unless you've personally visited the group they may potentially go to, you have no guarantee as to the biblical quality of the teaching. You might be able to link them with other Christian scholars in their university but in this situation we just need to entrust the new believer to God 'being confident of this that he who began a good work in [them] will carry it on to completion until the day of Christ Jesus' (Phil. 1:6).

Some of those working among students in UK may be able to help with contacts in China. (See appendix.)

Above all, Chinese who have become Christian while abroad need prayer. Pray that they grow in their new faith and find fellowship.

Guidelines in Summary

- Pray for God's guidance and specific leading in making contacts
- Prepare by reading about modern China, Chinese culture, the history of Christianity in China, Chinese Communism, and Christian apologetics. If you have access to the web, keep up to date by reading the China section of a news website. You can also read various newspapers online including the English language version of the People's Daily!
- Take the initiative in welcoming, befriending and trying to meet some needs of Chinese students and their families
- Show genuine love in a two-way friendship; don't just take your Chinese friends to Christian meetings
- Learn to understand their background and the pressures they face in China as well as in their new environment overseas
- Share the gospel with sensitivity, remembering their possible political status here, and avoiding aggressive 'hard sell' techniques.

Six

Appendix

Suggested Reading

<u>China: General</u>

Jung Chang, *Wild Swans – Three Daughters of China* (Harper Collins) 1993

Fox Butterfield, *China – Alive in the Bitter Sea* (Coronet) 1982

Zhang Xinxin and Sang Ye, *Chinese Lives: An Oral History of Contemporary China* (Pantheon) 1987

G Barme & J Minford, *Seeds of Fire: Chinese Voices of Conscience* (Noonday Press) 1989

John Gittings, *The Changing Face of China: From Mao to Market* (OUP) 2005

Xinran Xue, *The Good Women of China: Hidden Voices* (Vintage) 2003

Glenn Myers, *China Briefings* (Authentic) 2006

China Resources Handbook (OMF) 2005

<u>China: Religion</u>

C K Yang, *Religion in Chinese Society* (University of California Press), 1961

Tony Lambert, *The Resurrection of the Chinese Church* (OMF/Harold Shaw) 1994

Danyun, *Lilies Amongst Thorns: Chinese Christians Tell their Story* (Sovereign World) 1991

Tony Lambert, *China's Christian Millions* (OMF and Monarch Books) 2006

Marxism / Maoism

Scarfe & Sookhdeo, *Christianity & Marxism* (Paternoster Press) 1982

Dr Li Zhisui, *The Private Life of Chairman Mao* (Random House) 1994

D J Munro, *The Concept of Man in Contemporary China* (University of Michigan Press) 1977

Mark R Elliott, *Christianity & Marxism Worldwide: An Annotated Biography* (Institute for the Study of Christianity and Marxism, Wheaton Illinois) 1988

Benjamin Yang, *Deng – A Political Biography* (M.E. Sharpe) 1997

Jung Chang and Jon Halliday, *Mao* (Knopf) 2005

Whitney Stewart, *Mao Zedong* (Twenty-First Century Books) 2006

Christian Apologetics

Colin Russell, *Cross-Currents: Interactions between Science and Faith* (IVP) 1985

Derek Burke (ed), *Creation and Evolution* (IVP) 1985

Nigel M de S Cameron, *Evolution and the Authority of the Bible* (Paternoster) 1983

Prof R J Berry (ed), *Real Science, Real Faith: Sixteen British Scientists Discuss their Science and Faith* (Monarch) 1991

Richard Milton, *The Facts of Life: Shattering the Myths of Darwinism* (Fourth Estate) 1992

OMF Apologetic Literature

More than fifty booklets are in print in Chinese characters (some bilingual Chinese/English or Chinese translations of material already available in English elsewhere) on a wide variety of subjects. Key titles include:

'What is Christianity?'
'Religious Views of Famous People.'
'Bone of Contention'
'Modern Western Philosophy and Christianity'
'Chinese Culture and Christianity'
'Not a Superstitious Belief'
'Scientists Also Believe in God'
'What are the Advantages of Believing in Jesus?'
'Do Good People Need Jesus?'
'Testimonies of Chinese Intellectuals Abroad'
'Ten Principles for a Happy Marriage'
'Basic Bible Studies'

A series of 49 booklets which form a 'Theological Extension Programme for Mainland Chinese'. It is also available as a CD which includes a Chinese and an English Bible.

For a catalogue of the booklets available from OMF and to order them please contact emdir@omf.org.uk

These and other titles, as well as a range of cassette tapes, videos and CDs in Chinese (including the Jesus video) and bilingual New Testaments are available from OMF centres listed below and some other suggested sources.

Useful Contacts

UK and Ireland

OMF International: Ethnic Ministries Team
Station Approach, Borough Green, Sevenoaks, Kent, TN15 8BG UK
Tel. +44 (0)1732 887299
Email: omf@omf.org.uk
Web: www.omf.org.uk

OMF's Ethnic Ministries Team in the UK runs Church Training Days to enable British Christians to more effectively reach out to Chinese and other East Asians. For details of the current schedule or information on organising a training day in your area, please contact the Ethnic Ministries Team as above. The team can also give help and advice and speak at meetings.

Friends International
   3 Crescent Stables, 139 Upper Richmond Road, London SW15 2TN UK
   Tel: +44 (0)20 8780 3511
   Email: info@friendsinternational.org.uk
   Web: www.friendsinternational.org.uk

Friends International is a Christian mission agency which equips and motivates churches to reach international students for Christ. They organise training events and support a variety of activities in UK cities to welcome and befriend international students.

HOST UK
   1 Ardleigh Road, London N1 4HS
   Tel: +44 (0)207 254 3039
   Web: www.hostuk.org.uk
   Open: 10am to 4pm Monday to Friday

HOST UK enables adult international students at universities, colleges and on professional attachments in the UK, to visit for a day, a weekend, Christmas or another festival as guests in private homes, thereby helping the students to feel welcome in this country and promoting international friendship and understanding.

   HOST are not a Christian organisation but there is no bar on taking a student to church or sharing your faith with them. HOST are in need of many more homes to meet the demand of students wanting to visit British homes.

UCCF: The Christian Unions
　　38 De Montfort Street, Leicester LE1 7GP
　　Tel: +44 (0)116 255 1700
　　Email: email@uccf.org.uk
　　Web: www.uccf.org.uk

Chinese Overseas Christian Mission
　　2 Padstow Avenue, Fishermead, Milton Keynes
　　MK6 2ES
　　Tel: +44 (0)1908-234100
　　Email: bookroom@cocm.org.uk
　　Web: www.cocm.org.uk

COCM stock a large selection of books and Bibles in standard and simplified Chinese script as well as the Overseas Campus Magazine. The COCM website also provides details of Chinese Churches throughout Europe.

Overseas Campus Magazine
　　Web: www.oc.org

The Overseas Campus Magazine is produced by the Campus Evangelical Fellowship, which aims to preach the gospel of Jesus Christ; build up Christians; provide training for campus ministry workers; and mobilise Chinese to world evangelism. They work amongst intellectuals, providing literature, media resources and training.

No Frontiers
　　26-28 Lottbridge Drove, Eastbourne BN23 6NT, United Kingdom
　　Tel:+44 (0)1323 437723
　　Web: www.nofrontiers.org

No Frontiers provide literature and Bibles in a variety of languages.

Serve China Trust
    Telephone: +44 (0)115 928 3290
    Email: drwells@globalnet.co.uk

Serve China Trust provide a range of Chinese Bibles and Christian resources.

Ethnic Harvest Resources for Cross Cultural Ministry
    Web: www.ethnicharvest.org

Ethnic Harvest seek to serve and equip the Church for ministry in multi-ethnic society. Though they work mainly in North America, their website provides resources, stories and practical information.

China Horizon
    Web: www.chinahorizon.org/

China Horizon produces articles, books and apologetics material in Chinese and English.

Stephen Tong Evangelistic Ministries International
    Web: www.stemi.org

STEMI aims to evangelize people worldwide through large evangelistic rallies, theological training, the establishment of local churches and the production of literature and visual media. Stephen Tong was born in Mainland China but has travelled throughout the world preaching the gospel.

Christian Life Magazine
    Web: www.cclife.org

Christian Life Magazine is a quarterly publication aimed at Christians in Mainland China. They also produce 'Life and Faith', a magazine for Mainland Chinese seekers.

China Soul
    Web: www.chinasoul.org

China Soul aims to spread the gospel amongst Chinese. They produce a range of good quality videos and other materials.

Multi-Language Media
    Web: www.multilanguage.com

Multi-Language Media produce a range of Christian materials in other languages.

World Bible School – Chinese Characters
    Web: www.wbschool.org/chinesecharacters.htm

An evangelistic presentation looking at the origin of Chinese characters.

Contacts in Other English Speaking Countries:

OMF International
Australia:
PO Box 849, Epping, NSW 1710
Tel: 02 9868 4777 email: au@omf.net web: www.au.omf.org

Canada:
5155 Spectrum Way, Building 21, Mississauga, ONT L4W 5A1
Toll free: 1 888 657 8010 email: omfcanada@omf.ca web: www.ca.omf.org

Hong Kong:
PO Box 70505, Kowloon Central PO, Hong Kong
Tel: 852 2398 1823 email: hk@omf.net web: www.omf.org.hk

Malaysia:
3A Jalan Nipah, off Jalan Ampang, 55000, Kuala Lumpur
Tel: 603 4257 4263 email: my@omf.net web: www.my.omf.org

New Zealand:
PO Box 10159, Dominion Road, Balmoral, Auckland, 1030
Tel: 09 630 5778 email: omfnz@omf.net web: www.nz.omf.org

Philippines:
QCCPO Box 1997-1159, 1100 Quezon City, M.M.
Tel: 632 951 0782 email: ph-hc@omf.net web: www.omf.org

Singapore:
2 Cluny Road, Singapore 259570
Tel: 65 6475 4592 email: sno@omf.net web: www.sg.omf.org

UK:
Station Approach, Borough Green, Sevenoaks, Kent TN15 8BG
Tel: 01732 887299 email: omf@omf.org.uk web: www.omf.org.uk

USA:
10 West Dry Creek Circle, Littleton, CO 80120-4413
Toll free: 1 800 422 5330 email: omfus@omf.org web: www.us.omf.org

OMF International Headquarters:
2 Cluny Road, Singapore 259570
Tel: 65 6319 4550 email: ihq@omf.net web: www.omf.org

IFES
    Web: www.ifesworld.org

The International Fellowship of Evangelical Students works to establish a vibrant gospel witness among students in every nation. They work in 150 countries and should be able to provide help and resources wherever you are. Contact details for each country can be found on their website.

OMF International works in most East Asian countries, and among East Asian peoples around the world. It was founded by James Hudson Taylor in 1865 as the China Inland Mission. Our purpose is to glorify God through the urgent evangelisation of East Asia's billions.

In line with this, OMF Publishing seeks to motivate and equip Christians to make disciples of all peoples. Publications include:

- stories and biographies showing God at work in East Asia
- the biblical basis of mission and mission issues
- the growth and development of the church in Asia
- studies of Asian culture and religion

Books, booklets, articles and free downloads can be found on our website at www.omf.org

Christian Focus Publications

publishes books for all ages

Our mission statement –

STAYING FAITHFUL

In dependence upon God we seek to help make His infallible Word, the Bible, relevant. Our aim is to ensure that the Lord Jesus Christ is presented as the only hope to obtain forgiveness of sin, live a useful life and look forward to heaven with Him.

REACHING OUT

Christ's last command requires us to reach out to our world with His gospel. We seek to help fulfil that by publishing books that point people towards Jesus and help them develop a Christ-like maturity. We aim to equip all levels of readers for life, work, ministry and mission.

Books in our adult range are published in three imprints.

Christian Focus contains popular works including biographies, commentaries, basic doctrine and Christian living. Our children's books are also published in this imprint.

Mentor focuses on books written at a level suitable for Bible College and seminary students, pastors, and other serious readers. The imprint includes commentaries, doc-trinal studies, examination of current issues and church history.

Christian Heritage contains classic writings from the past.

Christian Focus Publications Ltd,
Geanies House, Fearn, Ross-shire,
IV20 1TW, Scotland, United Kingdom
info@christianfocus.com
www.christianfocus.com